The Life Dyslexic

Palewell Press

The Life Dyslexic

Poems by Philip Burton

The Life Dyslexic

First edition 2022 from Palewell Press,
www.palewellpress.co.uk
Printed and bound in the UK

ISBN 978-1-911587-62-0

The cover design is Copyright © 2022 Camilla Reeve

The front cover and back cover photos of Philip Burton are Copyright © 2022 Philip Burton

A CIP catalogue record for this title is available from the British Library.

Acknowledgements

Grateful thanks to Dr Ellen Reynor for appraising this pamphlet in the context of her extensive research into dyslexia as Assistant Professor at Dublin City University, her love and appreciation of poetry, and her expertise as a teacher of young children. Her detailed analysis of these poems is extremely supportive and encouraging.

A GAME NOT PECULIAR TO CAT AND MOUSE was published in #29 of Work Town Words.
AGAINST THE STREAM was shortlisted in the 2017 Segora poety competition, and won Third prize in the 2018 Cruse Lines poetry competition, Arundel.
AROUND WE GO is published in the geography-themed Allegro Poetry Magazine #27, March 2021.
CARVE A NAME FOR YOURSELF is published in coverstorybooks Line Breaks #1.
FALSE MEMORY won Third prize in the Hastings Litfest poetry competition 2019.
HEAD OF THE RIVER is in Weyfarers # 11, Autumn 2011.
I'LL WAIT HERE was published by Orbis # 123, Autumn 2002.
OXYGEN is included in The Ver Prize 2022 competition anthology.
SOLDERING ON was published in The Cannon's Mouth Quarterly #82, December 2021.
THE FIRST BIRD OF DYSLEXIA received a commendation in The Poetry Society Stanza Poetry competition, 2020. The judge was Heidi Williamson.
THE KISS CUBE is included in Work Town Words # 26, 2021.

THE OLD GREY PENCIL TEST is published in Work Town Words # 25, 2021.

Dedication

I dedicate this poetry to those, worldwide, who are dyslexic, including other dyslexic members of my extended family: Michael, Katy, Patrick. Paul, Joel, and Dominic, and to those who tutor, teach and give emotional and other support, and finally to the dedicated researchers who seek a scientific understanding of dyslexia and other neurodiverse conditions.

Contents

Introduction

Few teachers understood dyslexia back in the 1960's. It is now known that dyslexia is inbuilt, lifelong, and goes much wider than reading and writing difficulties; as a child, I was forgetful, disorganized, constantly late, a day-dreamer who made little progress.

As can be imagined, life was hard straight away at school in 1950, but I'm sure that having me as a pupil (along with forty-five other children crowded in a small classroom) made life ultra-hard for my teachers! I wore the dunce's cap, received the dunce's slap (daily), and then progressed, with great relief, at the age of nine, to the rejects group, which was left to its own quiet devices.

The poems look back more fondly on my time at Technical High school, and my reactions to teachers as they struggled, to either encourage or to force me to read and write, and how the colourful influence of some imaginative and enlightened men and women, who bravely tried out unconventional ways such as drama games, word lists, chemical symbols, and cursive writing, allowed me, exhaustingly, to build a neurone bridge to the frontal lobes of my brain.

MEMORY IS WHERE LIFE IS LIVED

Kevin Horsley

Head of the River

Seated near the Bowland brook
teased by runes of wrinkled shade
I was in class again

counted as one to whom no regard
was best given – *dyslexic* we'd say now,
shiftless then.

Nibs always bent, blots ruled okay.
Because I could not write, my heart hurt;
my backside too.

What saved me at school
were the high windows – square kites –
steadfast blue visited by white.

I understood Kent's River Stour –
sailed my mind's eye along it each day
from Westmarsh to Durnock.

If only they'd ask me to read aloud
its cordovan banks, hump-neck bridges,
slow cursive bends.

Paper words – second nature to my peers –
were rivers too, oxbow islands,
inlets with no landing-stage.

False Memory

... of when the ocean froze,
January, Ramsgate, nineteen sixty-three

Reach back. Surely I walked on the sea,
watched shoals of codling beneath my feet,
shook the claws of comatose lobsters,
blew snow off a conger, took the curves
of a broken wave for a Humpback whale,
heard the crack, slid, inhaled the ocean.
Reach forward. I can study the process –
how glials and neurones hook, gaff
fish out images for the grey aquarium.
Harbour mullet are such dull truth.
Mixed species dart this way and that:
mermaid, man-ray, Portuguese man-of-war,
sunshade, brinkmanship, *jugendherberge*...
Floated notions become miniature oceans
and they freeze even as I swim.
Thin ice collapses in the near distance
but I didn't drown on the beach walk.
My brain digs deep for a snowball
to scupper the runcible paper boat
of the story I launched, but it survives.
I did venture out on the ice.
And I did see the split widen in such a way
that there would be less credence
in maintaining I merely ambled back
on the way to visit a papier-mâché whale
in a modest Science museum.
Ice doom is what stuck, and I've hunted,
like an Inuit or a Polar bear, for any hint
of sky, somewhere to climb out.

ALPHABET SOUP WAS ALL I COULD MAKE

Ode on my 1951 Room

A feather had climbed through
the pattern of bars on my pillow.
Brave little quill. Painted letters
on alphabet blocks were not go-getters
at all. I liked things which moved
at the very slightest touch:

Lilliputian lace on the sills, pre-war
newsprint informing a drawer;
candlewick straining the trestle bed;
floorboards that breathed or died
with the falling gale or the rising tide;
lathe-turned toys in a ripe apple box:

diablo, skittles, whipping tops;
orange box of tiny cars: racing green,
bluebell blue, mustard yellow;
a leaning crane of loose Meccano;
gold-framed granddad lost in amber
having his smile become my own;

the slow march of ocean by the window;
the clock forever stopped, the curtain torn;
ancient roses letting their perfume up
till it spills across my yawn;
and Mother putting her head round the door.
I wish I could read her. I wish I could read.

The First Bird of Dyslexia

Morning has Broken, said the hymn
like the first morning; and (for me)
was unreadable even when pounded
out with heavy hammers
mor- / -ning / has / bro- / -ken

Teacher would perform the trick
of lifting a sound and a sherbet lemon
from a high shelf – *mor*, he would say –
cracking the sweet with his teeth
now you, now you...
                    – *ning* he would say
now you, now you, NOW YOU...

Each bit spoke for itself, I was told;
he showed his tongue and sweet fragments.
MOR- crack! -NING / HAS / BRO- crack! -KEN
a spine-touching nosedive of sound
scattering hanks of itself on the road outside.
Blackbird has spoken like the first bird
okay, but my spoke had a missing bicycle.

Nothing screamed from the page;
even when scratched by an adult fingernail
mor- couldn't talk, *-ning* had no bell.
I couldn't conceive of them leaping through eyes
into the brain, and out of the throat.

I hosted a dream of shapes and cyphers
that whispered, sneezed, clanged and blared
but none of them had any name, or if they did,
it constantly broke, broke again
like the first morning.

When told I was lazy or dull,
springing fresh from the Word
I perched my face on the loops and ascenders
of the wrought iron gate of the school
till morning mended.

The Kiss Cube

Before the age of twelve
the sole word
I was guaranteed
to read
was printed in red
on a silver cube
in the kitchen.

A throw of this die
always got me
two zeros and a kiss.

Why was I successful
in shiny 3d, but dumb
to anything inked on white?

Dyslexia is individual.
One word
was all the straw
I could grasp.

OXO spelled hope.

In Other Words

words took off in the air

sandwich board
cricket pad
smock and painting
easel, railing
tumbling after
scarf and garter
spindly twig
corn pad, bin lid
ten pence
head-dress
torn vest
hayseeds
loose beads
pram hood
toffee wrapper
plastic anchor
all were flung
by the hurricane
that came
and stopped me reading.

THE WISE WARDERS

A Good Word

Bypassing The Church of Saint Hugh
the whole school famously hurried
straight to dinner at The Parish Centre
but, if it rained, we'd take sanctuary –
   be let free like incense
     and raise faces
        to high windows

where orange coronas outglowed
the stone carpets and dubious benches.
Miss said, *Make sure you respect the saints.*
Heaven knows, the feast on view
   was party time
     and us kids were up
        for joining them

I'm a martyr to daydreams.
Saint Hugh went further, deep into prayer.
Going home to Lincoln Cathedral
he once rode clean past
   his own South-West Tower.
       I know that feeling.

I've ridden past Maths
a few times. Woke in Geography.
Saints may be there ahead of us
but on Saint Hugh's day
Miss Waite put lips to my ear.
Good to be different, she said.

Against the Stream

When the sun gets up, my street
is in my pocket. I lord it over cars.
I wave regally to flowers and don't guess
that they bow to the slightest breeze.
I shrink at school. *You must grow!*
screams Mrs Head. I will then —
only shorter. *Three sums. Begin!*
Where do subtracted bits go?

I play board rubber on the way home —
lose the day's facts in one fell swish.
I'm a grub fallen from lettuce
to kitchen sink. I swim to my room.
Round the bend, the sharp day
sees the bedroom light click off.
I hug the pane of the window
until my eyes become the glass.

The moon harvests the clouds,
scoops each glint from the field.
A branch? No, a fish in a beak
trying to find the current of the stream.

Perhaps it will, when it's older.
I purse my body, pillow my talk
and dive dive dive till the dawn
again broadens my shoulders.

Woodwork

Spelling tests don't cut much wood.
Can't read. Won't read. But you'll do.

Ask them in your English lesson
a proper, time-honoured question
like: cherry, elm, rosewood, maple –
which would make the better table?

They'll plump for one. They'll be wrong!
You'll say, Each would do the job
                  in its own sweet way.

I'll not castigate your spelling.
I'm more a spoken man myself, happy if you're telling
plank from batten, board from scantling.
Timber speaks for itself. Scent and feel, feel and scent:
mahogany beading, beech-wood dowel.

I think that I shall never see a thing as beautiful
as this wood-shaving.

Carve a Name for Yourself

a woodwork teacher's advice to a dyslexic child

Book words can resemble ghosts
or be like pressed flowers –
memorials to meadows lost
    down drains and under houses.

Although print has much to teach us,
letter shapes demand a solid base
as when the characters
are carved from blocks of linden wood –
not pared down to petty stains
all too flimsy on the page
    for anything but a passing glance
from one who strains to read.

Words spring from throat and hands
clay and wedge, chisel and mallet.
Hold that thought. Feel the power
in your fingers and palms.

Footnote – A doctor's note gave our woodwork teacher
permission to smoke in the classroom; he had been a
prisoner of war in Japan.

Soldering On

He was not a teacher, or so he claimed,
more a welder, solderer of concepts.
Metal's my first. Fixer's my surname.

He sensed my dyslexia was to blame.
Vocabulary is what my flux wets.
He was not a teacher, or so he claimed

but made words stick onto the brain
like silver solder, glue, or brass rivets.
Metal is my first. Fixer is my surname.

We'd carry a list of technical names
us kids. Pointing at one he'd say, *Let's*...
He was not a teacher, or so he claimed

but workshop words would jump alive.
We did them. They became precepts.
Metal's my first. Fixer's my surname.

*It's what I do. Here and now. Ends
are all made to meet with perfect success.*
He was not a teacher, or so he claimed.
Metal's my first. Fixer's my surname.

The Old Grey Pencil Test

Mister Bentine's room unnerved kids
with its mess tins of needle-sharp pencils,
big-time drawing boards,
and war surplus French curve stencils.

Heavy weaponry. I surrendered
myself, but my drawing proved invisible.
No, son, round up some force.
He gave me paper on which to doodle.

That's better. Open your shoulders,
lean down on the job. That's a sizable
improvement. Primary report
claims you're blind to any words at all.

Scribbles are my tea leaves. Verve
shows a hunger; I can foretell
from these livewire lunges of yours
you are going to be teachable.

Tableaux A Go Go

In 1961 Miss Wright, our young teacher, came back from
Juan-les-Pins having been to the nightclub Whisky a Go Go,
one of the first disco dancing places, and had seen how
children struggling with spelling might be helped.

The essence of her method was to play
Otis Redding's Sitting on the Dock of the Bay.
She'd call out RIM THE GYM and we'd squat
with backs to the wall bars, eager, alert.
GO, she would yell, and we'd scramble
to make the G and the O, without tangles
or unwieldy limbs. Come on letters, go to town!
Hit the deck dancing, then freeze your position
flat on the floor (as will Torville and Dean
at the end of Bolero, thirty-three years on).
Head to tail, like literate sardines, we'd glow,
lay and listen to Otis or Elvis, proud to know
we could spell at least the one word GO.
When calm came, we'd take turns to climb
and read ourselves. We'd made an isocheim –
a line on a map, first laid down in Juan-les-Pins.
Great to be sittin' when the evenin' comes
body full of words, echoes of sea and psalms.

In a Short Form

remembering Miss Elizabeth Steadman

She was quick to praise the way
I knew the first and last letters of a name
such as William The Conqueror. She gave me
carte blanche to put Wm The Cr

Nothing wrong at all, she said.
I try on a hat, I can't see my head.
I can't drive a car, but can work the doors.
I can lick seaside rock, of course,
without reading the peppermint word
B L A C K P O O L locked inside.

History was a breeze, after that, for me.
I could bookend the kings: Ge 1, Ge2, Ge3
and label the explorers: Dd Le, and St of the Ac
and Miss Ted would always decode it.
I worked inwards from there. *You're a true historian.*
You've hit on a system.

Oxygen

Aged 11 in a Chemistry lesson

Try again, try again
try again try again, what have
I just said? Spell *oxygen*
no not *o-g-z—o—j—e—n*!

Words are long grass.
Teacher stands, I crawl –
my nose impeded by stems.
She breathes from a
different place to me –
not *oksijun* but oxygen
not *ochsheejin* but oxygen
not *oxogen* but oxygen.

Reading is like breathing,
she says, but through
your little eyes. She mimes,
threads a needle
lean and silver. I pretend
to take it, stitch the long grass
flat, try see what she sees
on the warm horizon.

I overhear her say to staff,
He's a little open star
with his diamond cascade
of wildly glittering guesses!

My brain the tail of a comet?
I go round on a regular basis
but more than this
I secretly please her;

she can't understand me
well enough to tell me straight.
Chemistry is plain sailing though –
oxygen being O.

Mister Karr

Mister Karr was not worried by spelling
the way some others were. He'd seen worse
than a missing L in the scribble of war.

Spell away, spell away, I won't be telling
you off if your *Phisicks* has a k . I'm less
than bothered, as long as you nibble the kore

of Archimedes Principle and start revealing
an overflow of zeal, the odd bright guess,
an arking independence of mind. Eureka!

THE ANCIENT REGIME

From Two Teachers Talking

after a spelling test – a found poem

If Burton were more lithe
he could take up limbo dancing
where a low mark wins the prize.

Ode on a Garden Cane

Hold hard, my fine unfussy bamboo son,
    you clever stick – with such remembered feel –
reveal how come that somehow it's arisen
    you have the tensile strength to rival steel.
No timber, concrete, brick of kilned earth
    is uncrushable as you, but now, aglow
        in garden sun, you're not the mighty god
    to whom I bowed at school, my shirt-tail shown –
and took the swish I knew would burn
        a rebel badge of honour one inch broad.

Of late you prop an old boy's runner beans.
    As patient as an empty gun you wait
the roulette spin of social ways and means
    to send you flicking back to castigate
backside, hand, and mind – to crudely cap
    some child's bravura go at having fun.
        The shadows cower Back Birch Lane.
    The tender stems of love? to kingdom come.
Instead, the leather belt, the hawse, the cat,
        paddle, slipper, strap, are back again.

Miss Callas

My handwriting shrank in Religion
to an almost flat earthquake trace.
I'd pretend I could read each atom

but in truth I'd memorised a ton
of stuff whispered across by the guy
next to me. Miss was keen

to have me read what I'd written.
Yes, Miss, I can do that, Miss, I lied.
She took time to arrange herself to listen.

I parroted off the session notes
by heart. She sighed. *Clever child.*
See you in detention.

A Game Not Peculiar to Cat and Mouse

CAT
Kat

MOUSE
mows

Pulling the wool again
                is not acceptable.
I'd expect a better score from a vegetable.
No-one gets nought on ten.
A chimp could do more.
Use the memory store
            between your sideburns, Burton.

Okay, I'm going to write them down FOR you.

cat

mouse

If you get them wrong in TEST 3
you will be the mouse consumed by the cat
                which will be ME.

Around We Go

This is not Art, not a race, or done free.
Here is paper for tracing accurately.
You'll see your country through it, softened
to grey. Pencil-in the coastline. More
pressure, please; but control your passion.

Flip like a pancake, and see where you've been;
it shows clearly but cloudily through.
Go round the line again, even and crisp.
Turn over the paper. Use your left claw
to hold it firm. Scribble. That's an invitation!

Practical tasks extended to Geography
and the "map pen" was de rigueur;
its tapered nib, thin as two sewing pins,
would be dipped in ink, set to draw
over the pencil borders of home nations.

I made an accurate stab (at least for me).
I kept up, did a thorough Cooks Tour
but rendered England back to front. It was binned.
Dyslexic reversal was not known at this address.
The teacher drew out his cane.

THE GET OUT OF JAIL CARD

I'll Wait Here

Punishment stopped after a while. Benign neglect was tried. Sent to the back of the class to be ignored more easily, I had a great view of a nearby garden.

The dizzy iron of the gate
is drunk on snowdrop wine.
Tansy blurs the capstones
of the high retaining wall.
I straighten my clothes,
undress my senses, prepare to be
the cloud-wide courtyard
sprung with pools and sharp reflected smiles.
Mark my hours with terracotta urns
of rhizomes, and let me be the glad sleep
of bamboos, ferns and variegated grasses.
When Spring comes:
each second a primrose,
each minute a pale daffodil.
And when the twelve hours are done
it will be summer.

Contact

The benefits of cursive writing, particularly for students
with dyslexia have been noted for several years.

Picking up a pen wasn't hard.
A squiggle on the page was okay to do.
Locked in a distant country
were b, d, and p, (to name just a few).
Hercules would have struggled
with a thirteenth labour –
humping leaden letter shapes
uphill to the Brocca's Areas
in my front lobe.

When joined writing arrived
on the syllabus,
the snakes uncoiled from my legs;
I leapt from the chair of forgetfulness.
Cursive script freed me
to wiggle, flow, engage with the sky
safe in my roller coaster cart,
strapped in, alert, vivified.
At last, a main support structure,
smooth as the meaning of words,
dropped into place.

SUPPLEMENT

My take on Dyslexia

We are all different, but talking comes naturally, so that's generally okay. Reading and writing were invented, not so long ago in the great scheme of things, on a "one size fits all" basis; and that's the problem, but not an unsolvable one. Spectacles are an example of something tailored to meet individual needs, and dyslexia can be managed for the individual by special instruction and support. We can adapt to it, be shown ways through, even seem to grow out of it, but dyslexia is part of who we are.

As early as 1925 it was known that a significant group of reading problems are unrelated to a child's general ability, health record, and social background, yet failure to read and write continued to attract verbal abuse, public shaming (e.g. by having to wear a "dunce's cap"). Corporal punishment in schools continued till 1986.

Research has made strides. We now know that there is most likely a genetic component to the condition. In my own extended family, seven of us are dyslexic: Michael my son, Katy, Patrick. Paul, Joel, Dominic, and myself. There are visual *and* hearing aspects of the condition and this means that various teaching methods and technologies need to be tried to find the best and most effective for the individual learner.

Enlightened teachers, to whom I am eternally grateful, sensed that reading problems are found equally among rich and poor, men and women of every ethnicities, and in all languages, and will occur in children of all intelligence levels. Even today, sadly, approximately half of all people serving time in prison are dyslexic, compared to ten percent of the general public.

On the plus side, many dyslexics become high achievers; many musicians and artists are dyslexic. Dyslexic poets include W.B. Yeats, and Benjamin Zephaniah. There are a number of dyslexic strengths: advanced reasoning, pattern spotting, lateral thinking, communication skills, and data analysis. Research undertaken by *Made by Dyslexia* finds that eighty percent of successful dyslexics attribute their success to being dyslexic, whereas only three percent of the general public, and very few teachers, are aware that there are any advantages to being dyslexic. A recent book *This is Dyslexia* by Kate Griggs (Vermilion-Penguin 2021) is the definitive guide to the untapped power of dyslexic thinking and its vital role in our future.

Your doctor can give a referral for dyslexia testing by specialists who use a variety of reading assessments and instruments, including the Lindamood Test (for sound and phonetics), the Woodcock Johnson Achievement Battery, and the Grey Oral Reading Test among others to detect dyslexia. The British Dyslexia Association (BDA) developed The Adult Dyslexia Checklist. Further information can be found at http://dyslexiahelp.umich.edu/answers/faq and from The BDA.

Philip Burton

Time-Line

1877 – 1883: The condition of "word blindness" was identified and the word dyslexia was soon in use.

1920: The International Dyslexia Association (IDA) began to develop services in America.

1962: The first reference is made to dyslexia in the UK Parliament.

1970: Macdonald Critchley wrote *The Dyslexic Child* (William Heinemann Medical Books) Revised edition ISBN: 9780433067016). A range of organisations began to be founded: Helen Arkell Dyslexia Centre (1971), the Dyslexia Clinic at Barts Hospital (1971), the British Dyslexia Association (1972), the Dyslexia Institute (1972), the Language Development Unit at Aston University (1973).

1975: The Bullock Report *"A Language for Life"* makes only brief reference to dyslexia.

1977: The Bangor Dyslexia Unit was founded at Bangor University.

1998: A state school head teacher in Lancashire had to "go private" travelling to Birmingham to have his son diagnosed as dyslexic. The child was then statemented as having Special Educational Needs (SEN), but no provision could be made until Secondary school.

2001: In Ireland, The Report of the *Task Force on Dyslexia*, commissioned by the Department of Education and Science, recommended the development of a strategic plan for the establishment of additional special classes in mainstream schools for students with specific learning difficulties.

2010 – 2015: Early diagnosis and intervention is the key to helping dyslexic children, yet the number of Educational Psychologists employed by local authorities in the UK fell by thirteen percent.

2019: The British Dyslexia Association say that schools are failing to diagnose at least eighty percent of dyslexic pupils. The DfE announced that thirty million pounds will be allocated to training more Educational Psychologists.

2021: A landmark book is published, titled This is Dyslexia: The definitive guide to the untapped power of dyslexic thinking and its vital role in our future, Kate Briggs, Vermilion-Penguin.

Philip Burton – Biography

Philip Burton has a love for readings and performance, developed through life as an English and Drama teacher, Lancashire head teacher, folksinger, actor, and multi-award-winning poet. He was also, for some years, a poetry practitioner who, as *Pip The Poet*, provided hundreds of poetry days for schools and also for adult learners.

Three hundred and ninety-five of Philip's poems have appeared in literary magazines since 1998, including PN Review, and Stand. His poems have been widely anthologized.

Philip recently won the First prize of £500 in the East Riding Festival of Words poetry competition; the chief judge was James Nash; there were 600 entries.

He received a Commended award in the Indigo Open Poetry Prize competition 2022, and has a poem in The Ver Prize 2022 competition anthology.

In 2019, Philip held four First prizes concurrently in poetry competitions: the National Arts Centre Jack Clemo, 2019; the Horwich Writers, 2018; the Sandwich (Kent) Poet of the Year, 2018; and the Barn Owl Trust, 2017. Philip also won Third prize both in the 2019 Hastings poetry competition, and in The Ware Poets open poetry competition 2020.

Philip is a member of the Ribble Valley Stanza, and of the Clitheroe Writers Group, and is Honorary President of Burnley and District Writers' Circle

Philip Burton's other poetry publications include *The Raven's Diary* (joe publish 1998), *Couples* (Clitheroe Books Press 2008), *His Usual Theft* (Indigo Dreams Press 2017), and *Gaia Warnings* (Palewell Press 2021).

www.philipburton.net

Palewell Press

Palewell Press is an independent publisher handling poetry, fiction
and non-fiction with a focus on books that foster Justice, Equality and
Sustainability. The Editor can be reached on
enquiries@palewellpress.co.uk